The Fun Book for Girlfriends

Other Books by Melina Gerosa Bellows

The Fun Book
The Fun Book for Couples
Wish
The Fun Book for Moms

The Fun Book for Girlfriends

102 Ways for Girls to Have Fun

Melina Gerosa Bellows

Andrews McMeel Publishing, LLC

Kansas City

ISBN-13: 978-0-7407-7954-1
ISBN-10: 0-7407-7954-0

Library of Congress Control Number: 2008936162

09 10 11 12 13 TWP 10 9 8 7 6 5 4 3 2 1

www.andrewsmcmeel.com

Attention: Schools and Businesses

Andrews McMeel books are available at quantity discounts with bulk purchase for educational, business, or sales promotional use. For information, please write to: Special Sales Department, Andrews McMeel Publishing, LLC, 1130 Walnut Street, Kansas City, Missouri 64106.

For Karen and Rebecca

Acknowledgments

Where would I be without my girlfriends? They've helped me through everything from my hilarious '80s bilevel haircut to horrendous heartbreak over the years. Their empathetic listening, enthusiastic coaching, easy laughter, and happy-to-oblige corkscrews have kept my crayons in the box, so to speak. So here I must thank: Rebecca Ascher Walsh, Karen Hamilton, Laura Quill, Kristin Starr, Mary Fehrnstrom, Annie Belt, Lindsey Truitt, Isobel Coleman, Barbara Graham, Gloria Nagy, Simone Rathle, and Michelle Pearson. *The Fun Book for Girlfriends* is in your hands thanks to my wonderful agent and friend Claudia Cross, a writer's dream team, editor and publisher Chris Schillig and Kirsty Melville, the awesome artistic talents of Linda Kettlehut, and the gracious help of Jill Yaworski. I would also like to acknowledge the loving support of my family: parents Suzi and Carl, sister Jenn and brother C.J., and especially my beloved little posse, Keith, Chase, and Mackenzie. How lucky I am to call myself your friend.

Introduction

....

Sometimes I feel invisible. The inner me, my connection to joy, evaporates beneath the layers of roles I play: wife, mother, and boss. This painful condition can creep over me before I even know it's happening. Luckily, I'm blessed with girlfriends who can spot it a mile away.

"Hon, how 'bout a vacation?" suggests my friend Barbara over dinner. She knows I am feeling as see-through as Saran Wrap. "Can you and the hubby get away? You don't look so good."

"Two small problems with that," I remind Barbara. I'm talking about my twenty-two-month-old son and five-month-old daughter—neither of whom get my jokes. These days I spend almost all my time either working hard at my job or with them, hence no one gets my clever *Sex and the City* references, self-deprecating fat jokes, or hilarious one-liners. I suspect that being constantly alone inside my inside joke may be one of the leading causes of my debilitating condition.

"I'm giving you an assignment," Barbara announces bossily. "Go away for a long weekend. What you need is some *fun*."

I'm no stranger to the powerful, provocative, and even healing power of fun. Fun first came to my rescue when I was single. My knight in shining armor, fun never let me down even when my blind dates did. Back then, fun was a single girl's best friend. Possible anytime, anywhere, even when I least expected it, fun was a Zen master when it came to reducing stress, a zippy shortcut to living in the moment, and a stealth bomber to life's cruelest indignities.

Just when I was getting the hang of things—riding around in ragtops with my girlfriends, perfecting the dirty martini, and amusing myself by using my ex-boyfriend's favorite T-shirt to clean the bathroom floor—everything changed. I fell in love.

The fun I was having when I was single instantly doubled when I

met Keith. We kissed our way through movies and traveled the globe like rock stars, thanks to his job as the editor of a travel magazine. But it didn't matter if we were in the basement doing the laundry. As long as we were together, we were happy. After all, what could be more fun than falling in love?

Fun, like love, grows exponentially when shared. So after a couple of years of marriage, Keith and I decided to start a family. It took years of shots, pills, and doctor's appointments, but the effort paid off. I delivered a healthy baby boy we named Chase. Then, less than six months after Chase's birth, I was preggers again, without the help of modern medicine!

Shock, panic, delight, and every other emotion zinged around inside of me as if I were a human pinball machine. I had barely gotten the hang of our first little guy, when his party-crashing sister, Mackenzie, burst on the scene. Within seventeen months I was the mother of two. I had psychological whiplash to say the least. When I last checked, I wasn't capable of getting pregnant.

Admitting to myself that I had no idea how to transition into this demanding new stage in life, plus do my job as a magazine editor and keep my marriage from becoming platonic, I reached out to my friends for help, advice, and anything else that could get me through.

My e-mail SOS was first met with hilarious one-liners: "Rubberband your kitchen sink sprayer so when your kids turn on the water they get squirted in the face," wrote Mary Fehrnstrom, mother of three. "Always good for a laugh!"

Laura Quill, Tiburón mother of five, suggested that I divide and conquer: "Steal your kids away for one-on-one dates. Take them to the library or Starbucks and let them pick out a pastry and play cards, or go for nature walks and look for treasures. Nothing fancy, just make each child feel special."

Thanks to my friends, motherhood *was* getting easier. But still, where was *I* in all of this sippy cup madness? Somewhere along the way, my inner fun girl disappeared. Then, during my umpteenth trip to the grocery store, I spotted a bumper sticker on a minivan that proclaimed, "If Momma Isn't Happy, Nobody's Happy."

As Oprah would say, it was an "aha" moment. I made a dinner date with Barbara for that night. I needed someone to laugh at my jokes. But by the time I got to the dinner, my sense of humor had evaporated like the rest of me.

"I'm serious," she says. "Do it. Go on a vacation."

I look into my friend's concerned eyes, and I see the truth: I have to take a break; I'm not Superwoman. I sigh, trying to imagine myself getting out of Dodge.

It always strikes me as unnatural when flight attendants instruct passengers to put on their own oxygen masks before assisting their children, in case of emergency. It feels similarly unnatural to strike out on my own, but I call my go-to travel buddy, Rebecca, anyway. Our past excursions have included a luxurious last-minute weekend at the Ritz in Madrid and sojourns in the south of France. I suggest we go for a few days to Cal-a-Vie, a spa in Southern California that features hiking, meditation, and treatments galore.

"A *spa?*" she asks. I can practically hear her nose wrinkling in disdain over the phone. (Did I mention that she's skinny and perfect looking, and has never been on a diet in her life? I know. And I like her anyway.)

"OK," she says. "But only because you sound so tired." That's her euphemism for my lost self.

She prepares for the trip by eating and drinking herself silly, and calling me from every checkpoint from the bar to the cheese counter at Dean and Deluca.

"I'm hungover and bloated," she calls to inform me en route to the airport. Because I live in Washington and Rebecca lives in New York, we plan to meet in California. "Now I'm ready for the spa," she adds.

Me, on the other hand, I'm not so ready. I'm so discombobulated that I go to the wrong airport and miss my flight. When I eventually reach my destination, I'm so exhausted that I sleep for twelve straight hours.

The next day at the spa's pool, we meet some women who share Rebecca's restlessness with the spartan spa life. Within a millisecond, we hatch a bad girl breakout to buy supplies for a secret cocktail party.

Back in a new friend's room, happy hour starts, and almost immediately the sad stories start pouring out. Although these women look like they have everything I don't—beauty, money, quiet, and oodles of time to enjoy it all—they don't seem particularly happy. As we say

good-bye for the evening, I realize something obvious: Fun does not come one-size-fits-all. Forget what you *think* will make you happy; you have to keep trying until something *feels* good.

The next morning I rise at 5:30 for a nature hike, which is not Rebecca's idea of fun, so she sleeps in. By the time the ninety-minute trek ends, I feel exhilarated by the spectacular beauty of nature, the rigorous exercise, and time alone with my thoughts. It was not a mistake to take a fun time-out and come here, I tell myself. I can actually feel my spirit recharging. I will be a better wife, mother, friend, everything, because of this quickie girlfriend getaway.

After the hike, I'm in the library sipping herbal tea when one of the other guests joins me.

"So, where's your beautiful daughter?" she asks.

"At home with my husband," I say, confused.

"Rebecca went home?" she asks.

I am older than Rebecca. But only by three years.

I mumble something incoherent and excuse myself.

Yeeeouch!

Stinging from the fact that I actually *do* look

as bad as I feel, I find my way to the spa's white-pebbled meditation labyrinth. I stomp through it angrily and briskly, enjoying the crunch beneath my running shoes. Maybe I'm better off being invisible, I think, mumbling zinger comebacks to the guest who had insulted me. I know I look crazy to anyone watching me.

Crunch, crunch. As I walk alone, focusing my thoughts simply on my feet hitting the earth, the zinger comebacks quiet enough for a truth to arise. There is something important I need to do. It's not losing weight, the usual item topping my to-do list, but reclaiming my MIA sense of humor. But how? I don't even know who I am anymore.

Our last day at the spa, Rebecca and I have a ninety-minute seaweed wrap together. We are scrubbed, slathered, and wrapped up in silver Mylar bags like burritos. I'm drifting blissfully between being awake and being asleep, when Rebecca murmurs, "Guess what?"

"What?" I ask, wondering what could possibly be so important to disturb this total Zen relaxation.

"I've gained six pounds in three days," she says.

"Well, at least you don't look like you could be my mother," I respond.

"What?" she asks.

"That lady from Toledo thought I was your mother," I say.

Rebecca guffaws so hard that she almost slides out of her burrito. I can't help it and start laughing, too. I laugh so hard that no sound comes out, and then I hear it—my bubble of invisibility pops, and just like you'd see in a cartoon, I'm suddenly my old self again.

It's a lesson I learn over and over in my life. Seaweed wraps and pampering soothe the body, but there's nothing like friendship to balm the weary soul.

And the best part about friendship is that, like any pure fun, it doesn't need to happen anywhere out of the ordinary. Friendship is democratically available to one and all. I decide right then and there to upgrade connecting with friends from the occasional treat to a daily priority, even if it's just a phone call or an e-mail.

My real "aha" moment is this: Like the oxygen masks on the airplane, friendship is the surest lifeline that can sustain a woman through life's raggedy

transitions, scary challenges, and inevitable heartbreaks. As I learned in the silver burrito, there may be no hardship in life that can't be lessened by a belly laugh with a best friend—especially when the humor is at your own expense with someone who knows and loves you well.

While my favorite women are scattered all over the country, I am proud to have amassed such a spectacular and jewel-like collection of friends. Over the last year, they have helped me in a plethora of ways. Annie leaves surprises on my desk—everything from a butterfly shirt from Anthropologie to plastic frogs for my kids that expand to ten times their size. Gloria will listen for hours while I upload a long, long, story and still make me feel like we've barely scratched the surface when we hang up. Simone knows just the right time to spontaneously invite me over for wine and cheese on a weeknight, and Lindsay is always up for an outing.

Like fine wine, the best friendships improve with age. My college friends—Karen, Kristin, Laura, Mary, Nancy, and Lisa—have such spectacular senses of humor, that after spending time with them I, too, look at the world as if it's a supremely funny place no matter what is going on in my own life. Whenever I spot something worth mentioning, say, a man with

a French pedicure next to me at the grocery store, I smile, telling my friends telepathically even before I can whip out my cell phone.

And the most amazing thing about friendship is that it is as fun to give as to receive. Connecting with friends in simple ways, like going out of my way to reschedule an appointment to be there for a friend who needs to talk, dropping off brownies for a frazzled new mom, or even leaving funny messages for friends, has cheered me up as much as the recipient.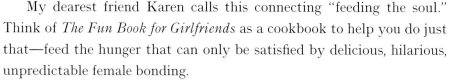

My dearest friend Karen calls this connecting "feeding the soul." Think of *The Fun Book for Girlfriends* as a cookbook to help you do just that—feed the hunger that can only be satisfied by delicious, hilarious, unpredictable female bonding.

What's your favorite flavor of fun with friends? Please e-mail me at mbellows@ngs.org so I can share your ideas online. In the meantime, turn the page and enjoy the soul food!

The Fun Book for Girlfriends

"Kidnap" your friend for her next birthday.

Prearrange for her to have the afternoon off. Pick her up, blindfold her, and take her to a mani-pedi. Go for free makeovers, and then meet the rest of the gang at her favorite café for drinks and appetizers. She'll have a day full of fun memories instead of a material gift she doesn't really need.

We do not remember days . . . we remember moments.

Cesare Pavese

*B*efriend women from different generations. Enjoy peeking at life through their *unique* perspectives.

$\mathscr{T}$he night that your friend has
been dumped, take her to the
swankiest spot in town. Secretly arrange
for the bartender to serve her a drink
sent from an anonymous admirer.

$\mathcal{T}$wo weeks before Christmas, when everyone
is really stressed out, host a tacky party (women only).
Ask each friend to dress in her tackiest outfit,
and bring a tacky appetizer (Jell-O mold, Cheese Whiz)
and a tacky gift (fur-lined teddy, lawn troll,
Santa Chia pet) for a white elephant grab bag.

Award prizes.

Play the

Booty Call Game

with a group of girlfriends.

Here's how it works: Give each friend the names of
three men; each friend must pretend to make booty calls
to the men in front of all of you. This works equally well
with movie stars (Johnny Depp, George Clooney, Brad Pitt),
men you all know from the neighborhood or office,
dead presidents, or fat comedians.

Have everyone bring some clothes, jewelry, and accessories that have inflicted buyers' remorse. Trade away and take turns accessorizing each other.

*F*ix up friends who can help each other with jobs or projects, or who you think may simply enjoy each other's company.

*I*f you and a friend
go to the same salon,
synch your hair appointments.
Bring *lattes* and the latest
fashion and *gossip* magazines.

When a friend is going through a transition or challenging time (birth of baby, loss of job, sickness in the family, bad day), bring her a home-cooked meal. Don't forget Mackenzie's Incredible Brownies.

Mackenzie's Incredible Brownies

4 oz unsweetened chocolate
1 lb sweet butter
4 eggs
2 cups sugar
2 tsp vanilla
1 cup sifted flour
12 oz package semi-sweet chocolate chips

1. Preheat the oven to 350°F.

2. Melt the chocolate and butter over low heat or in the top part of a double boiler. Let the chocolate mixture cool.

3. Insert steel blade into a food processor. Place the eggs in a work bowl and process until frothy. With the machine running, slowly add the sugar through the feed tube. Let the machine run several minutes or until the mixture is thick and lighter in color. Add the vanilla and flour, and turn on/off just until combined. Add the chocolate mixture and process until combined. Add the chocolate chips and turn on/off several times until mixed.

4. Transfer the mixture to a greased 9" x 13" x 2" pan and bake 25 to 30 minutes. Let the brownies cool before cutting.

When something bad happens to you,
tell as many friends as possible
(for some reason, this lessens the sting).

There is no wilderness like life without friends;
friendship multiplies blessings and minimizes
misfortunes; it is a unique remedy against adversity
and it soothes the soul.

Baltasar Gracián

Start a restaurant birthday club.

Have each friend write a fictitious letter from
someone in the birthday girl's life (her first boyfriend,
her mean gym teacher, her best friend from kindergarten).
Read them periodically during the celebration.

Do yoga as a group.

Beginners, set up your mats in the back of the class and when the going gets tough, giggle. Intermediate yoginis, do a weekend yoga retreat. Experienced yoginis, plan a pilgrimage to India.

The happiest business in all the world
is that of making friends.

Anne S. Eaton

At your next Christmas or New Year's Eve party, buy individual bottles of champagne and serve them to everyone with straws.

$\mathcal{M}$ake friends with the things that scare you, like uncertainty, being alone, or gaining weight. Like intimidating people at a cocktail party, these issues may have some very good information for you.

May there always be an angel by your side.

anonymous blessing

Meet a friend who lives in a faraway place for a weekend in a city where neither of you have been.

Never criticize a friend's boyfriend or husband,
even during a breakup.
(She'll have plenty of bad things to say about him herself.)

Life is the first gift,
love is the second,
and understanding the third.

Marge Piercy

Buy a friend the dollhouse/bike with streamers/
Partridge Family lunchbox she always wanted as a kid.

Google the lyrics to a friend's favorite song
and e-mail them to her.

$\mathcal{T}$ell your closest friends what you need from them. Be brave and politely make your request just as if you were telling a waiter how you like your steak.

The growth of friendship may be a lifelong affair.

Sarah Orne
Jewell

Hit the phone bar:

Unplug your life and pick up
the phone for a prearranged drink date
with a faraway friend
(bar snacks optional).

Intimacies between women often go backwards,
beginning in revelations and ending in small talk.

Elizabeth Bowen

22

*A*lways make your
friend's dog feel welcome, too.
Put out a water bowl and dog treats.

Meet a friend at a café or front porch and watch the world go by together.

*I*f a friend's *boyfriend* is perfect in every way except for those two-toned, weird sandals he wears, surreptitiously steal just one.

Whenever you are traveling and find
the perfect thing—an unusual scarf, dangling Indian earrings,
a delicious smelling candle—buy two: one to keep,
one to give away. Refer to them as your
"friendship earrings" (or whatever).

Happiness seems made to be shared.

Jean Racine

Road trip.

Rent a convertible with a close friend
and take a long drive out of town.
Call each other *Thelma* and *Louise*
as soon as you hit the highway.

Learn how to speak Italian with a friend.

Practice in Italian restaurants. Some key words to get you started:

vino : wine

si : yes

gnocci : gnocci

Il cameriere, lei ha di begli occhi : Waiter, you have beautiful eyes

Each friend represents
a world in us, a world possibly
not born until they arrive, and it
is only by this meeting that
a new world is born.

Anaïs Nin

$\mathcal{C}$asually mention to a friend's ex how thin/happy/in love the friend he dumped is. Report back to your friend how fat/bald/fired her ex is.

(Exaggeration allowed.)

$\mathscr{F}$or your high school buddies, create a playlist of hits from the year you graduated. Plan a conference call to reminisce about the cliques, nerds, and studs from high school.

(Don't skip reunions!)

We are friends for life.
When we're together the years fall away.
Isn't that what matters?
To have someone who remembers
how far you've come?

Judy Blume

$\mathcal{M}$eet friends for high tea at a fancy hotel.
Wear hats and order in English accents
and see if your waiter notices.

$\mathcal{F}$ind a mentor . . .
or someone to mentor yourself.

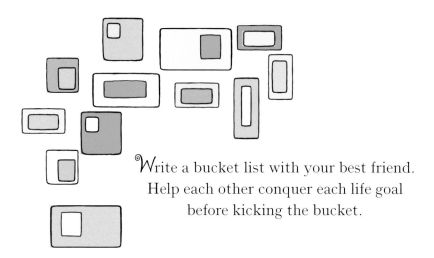

Write a bucket list with your best friend.
Help each other conquer each life goal
before kicking the bucket.

Think big thoughts, but relish small pleasures.

H. Jackson Brown Jr.

Send the funniest *New Yorker* jokes and
YouTube videos to your friends.

One can never
speak enough of the virtues,
the dangers, the power
of shared laughter.

Françoise Sagan

35

When one of your friends
has a birthday, surprise her with
breakfast at her place.
Bring *cappuccino*, *muffins*,
and *fresh flowers*.
No matter what her day holds,
she will have had a memorable morning.

$\mathcal{L}$earn the art of platonically flirting with other women.
Tell a friend she looks fabulous and be specific.
(The compliment *must* be sincere.)

Friendship is Love without his wings!

Lord Byron

Get rid of Aunt Mabel's ugly gravy boat
without guilt by hosting a china swap.
Everyone brings china they don't want anymore
and gets to take home something new.

Treat your best friends with your best manners. Use *pleases*, *thank-yous*, and *excuse mes*, so they feel like royalty.

When a friend gets that monthly edge in her voice,
ignore it and buy her the five-pound bar
of Belgian chocolate.

Get an old copy of *Color Me Beautiful* and discover
your "seasons." Go shopping at H&M for
T-shirts in your best colors.

Form a group of walking/running/dog walking/skipping buddies. Meet twice a week to solve world problems, gossip, and give each other advice as you exercise.

$\mathcal{T}$alk in plural whenever a friend is
going through something big.

For example:
"Here's what we can do about that."

$\mathcal{O}$n Valentine's Day, send all of your girlfriends funny cards with stickers and candy necklaces.

Celebrate a holiday with a friend
whose family is a different religion than yours.

God gave us our relatives;
thank God we can choose our friends.

Ethel Watts Mumford

$\mathcal{S}$ave up with your best friend to go on a fabulous, exotic trip like a safari in Africa.

Meet your funniest pal in a card shop.

Do your annual shopping for birthday cards, and be sure to share the funniest ones with each other.

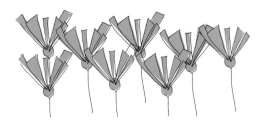

When tragedy strikes a friend, casually remind her of someone very *glamorous* who has faced a similar humiliation or challenge.

Go to a spa with your best friend.

Ten greats to try:

Cal-a-Vie, Vista, California

Floating Royal Taj Spa, Udaipur, India

Four Seasons Resort, Chiang Mai, Thailand

Maroma Resort and Spa, Quintana Roo, Mexico

Mauna Lani Spa, Kohala Coast, Hawaii

Mii Amo, a Destination Spa at Enchantment, Sedona, Arizona

Miraval Resort, Catalina, Arizona

Spa Montage, Montage Resort and Spa, Laguna Beach, California

Villas at Amangiri, Lake Powell, Utah

Wickaninnish Inn, Vancouver Island, Canada

Taking joy in life is a woman's best cosmetic.

Rosalind Russell

Take belly-dancing lessons
with a friend.

Once you perfect your shimmy
and snake arm moves, get jingly outfits
at the mall or in Morocco.

If you start feeling drained, you might need to weed out your garden of friends. Pull out those chokers, the energy vampires who leave you feeling exhausted. The new space in your "garden" will allow true friendships to blossom and create room to plant some new seeds.

Volunteer with a friend to do something that you both enjoy, such as walking dogs for the local branch of the American Society for the Prevention of Cruelty to Animals, mentoring underprivileged girls, or putting together care packages for the needy during the holidays. Or, sign up for the two-day Avon Breast Cancer Walk; sleep in tents and enjoy training together.

Even if you've grown apart from a friend and your lives have taken you in different directions, remember to always celebrate common ground. Laugh about the funny things you used to wear in high school or the terrible boss you both survived.

A friend is someone who understands your past, believes in your future, and accepts you today just the way you are.

anonymous

54

Always
tell your friend the truth.

(Unless the
question is
"Do I look fat?"
If yes, gently
guide her into the
black pants.)

$\mathcal{G}$o on a fashion safari
to the outlets.

Start a drumming circle with a group of girlfriends.
Take turns doing wild dance solos.
Dance solos mandatory.

Life is the dancer and you are the dance.
Eckhart Tolle

Girl date.

When you meet someone new and wonderful,
follow up with an invitation for a drink or lunch.

(Make sure you treat the first time.)

I think this is the beginning of a beautiful friendship.

from the film
Casablanca

$\mathcal{T}$ake turns with a friend organizing each other's closets. Or, as a birthday present for your friend, gather the pals and play personal shopper. Sit in the dressing room and help her find the season's outfits that look best on her.

Give your friend a Happiness Makeover.

Interview her about the twelve things she likes and hates about her life. Help her schedule more of the "likes" into her week, and brainstorm ways to change the things she doesn't like about her life.

Be happy.
It's one way of being wise.

Colette

Host a cheese party.

Ask each person to bring her favorite cheese
along with a new friend to introduce to the group.
Serve Rosemary and Pear Martinis using this recipe
from Susan Gage Catering. Makes 1 gallon.

1 (750 ml) bottle Grey Goose La Poire
1 (12 oz) bottle Stirrings Rosemary Martini Simple Syrup
1 (375 ml) bottle Poires Williams
3 (12 oz) cans pear nectar

Serve with a fresh sprig of rosemary.

Rent a limousine with a group of friends.
Get dressed up like movie stars,
and then go get fake eyelashes applied.
Go bar hopping and see if anyone notices.

$\mathcal{T}$ake turns with your friends helping each other plant container gardens to attract butterflies.

To know someone with whom you can feel
there is understanding in spite of distances
or thoughts unexpressed . . .
that can make this life a garden.

Goethe

Give your friend the ultimate present—
the gift of really listening.
Paraphrase and repeat back her most
salient points, so she knows you
truly understand her.

Resist the urge to give her advice until she asks you.

Coordinate a day off with a friend.

Go shopping, have lunch,
and then head to a chick flick matinee.

Start a book club and read Eckhart Tolle,
Pema Chödrön, Deepak Chopra, or any
favorite philosopher together.

Always check the sales rack
in your best friend's size, too.

Trouble is a sieve through which
we sift our acquaintances.
Those too big to pass through
are our friends.

Arlene Francis

When a friend is feeling fat,
make playlists for her to work out to.

Buy glamorous black-tie outfits
with your best friend.
Seek out invitations to glamorous events
so you can wear them.

$\mathscr{S}$tockpile beautiful little presents (candles, picture frames, jewelry) so you always have a gift on hand when a friend deserves something "just because."

A friend is a present you give yourself.

Robert Louis Stevenson

$\mathscr{P}$ride yourself on your eclectic, jewel-like collection of friends, appreciating each one for the sparkle she brings to your life.

Earth's crammed with heaven.

Elizabeth Barrett Browning

Always follow up the next day to ask how a friend's blind date/ presentation to the board/ parent-teacher conference went. Your *caring* interest in your friend's experiences always will be appreciated.

Go to Chanel with a friend and
try on *blazers* with *jeans*.
When you leave without buying
anything, casually mention that
you have so many at home,
you've decided to wait
for the next season.

Give a birthday shower:

Have friends chip in and buy the birthday girl
a colorful new shower curtain, towels, and bath mat,
plus yummy new shampoo, conditioner, and soap.

Go for a bra makeover with a friend.

Laugh when you hear her getting felt up
by the fitter in the dressing room.

Admit fault.

Say you understand the effect your actions
had on your friend.

Show that you are truly sorry.

Promise to fix the problem you caused and never do it again.

$\mathcal{B}$uy beautiful stationary and write letters to your friends. Remember the joyous arrival of snail mail?

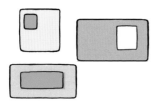

Start a cooking club
with your friends.

Each month, pick a new cookbook,
ask everyone to bring a dish, and meet
at a different person's home.
Have everyone play truth or dare
while enjoying the food.

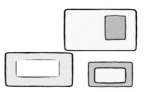

Tonight's Menu

Wendy . . . .
Georgette . . . .
Lucy . . . .
Nicola . . . .
Myra . . . .

Celebrate the gifts each friend has to offer.

Friendships do not come in one-size-fits-all.
Appreciate each friend's uniqueness, even if she isn't
perfect in every way.

There is space within sisterhood for likeness
and difference, for the subtle differences
that challenge and delight; there is
space for disappointment—and surprise.

Christine Downing

Download this *Girls Like Us* playlist,
and remind your friend to never listen to it
in male company:

"You're So Vain" by Carly Simon

"River" by Joni Mitchell

"It's Too Late" by Carole King

"Nobody Does It Better" by Carly Simon

"Big Yellow Taxi" by Joni Mitchell

"I Feel the Earth Move" by Carole King

"Anticipation" by Carly Simon

"Help Me" by Joni Mitchell

"So Far Away" by Carole King

"Haven't Got Time for the Pain" by Carly Simon

"Both Sides, Now" by Joni Mitchell

"Will You Love Me Tomorrow?" by Carole King

"You've Got a Friend" by James Taylor (because they all loved him)

Have one friend with whom
you share all of your most
embarrassing foibles. Make it into
a contest; whoever humiliates herself
the most, wins.

$\mathscr{R}$emember, your own body is the very best friend you will have in your lifetime. Who else would stick with you through thick and thin? Treat it with kindness, gratitude, and forgiveness.

Go hiking with a close friend.

$\mathcal{D}$evote yourself to the art of compassion.
Practice on friends and strangers daily.

Friendship is one heart
in two bodies.

Joseph Zabara

Revel in your *girl crushes*.

Everyone comes into your life for a season,
a reason, or a lifetime. Consider the women in your life
to be angels, each with a message, a mission,
or a gift.

It's up to you to figure out which.

*A*lways encourage your friends
to choose happiness.

Life is to be fortified by many friendships.
To love and to be loved is the
greatest happiness of existence.

Sydney Smith

Collect friends who make you laugh.

Never let a friend dial her ex
after she's had too many drinks.

Start a profile on Facebook.
Look up friends from long ago.

Plan a play date with
another mom and kids.

Swap kids in the car
so you can get to know them better.

Bonus:
They'll behave better.

$\mathcal{R}$esist the urge to judge another woman until you've walked a mile in her Manolos.

$\mathcal{S}$hare your husband/brother/teen to be her technology concierge.

$\mathcal{A}$lways call to ask your friend
what she'll wear to the big date/
interview/TV appearance.
Tell her she can borrow *anything*
from your closet or jewelry box.

Develop your friendship ESP.

When you are thinking about a friend,
get in touch to see if she's thinking about you, too.

However rare true love is, true friendship is rarer.

La Rochefoucauld

Keep a bottle of
good *champagne* in the fridge
so it's on hand to celebrate.
Open it for little successes
and celebrations as well as
the big ones.

$\mathcal{I}$nvite a tarot card reader
to your next friend's birthday.

Trade chores that you hate.

Polish your friend's silver jewelry
while she uploads your digital photos.

Have a meditation buddy.

Keep track of the synchronicities you notice in your lives.

Make and stay friends with the parents of your preschoolers' pals. You'll enjoy comparing ages, stages, and parenting mistakes while the kids grow up.

The best gift is being kind to yourself.

Never, ever speak to yourself less kindly
than you would your best pal.
(Even in the privacy of your own mind.)

Whoever is happy will make others happy too.

Anne Frank

Bake cupcakes with a friend.

Wrap them in a pretty shoebox and
spontaneously deliver them to a pal who's
down in the dumps.

Make your New Year's resolution to
celebrate one thing about/for/with one friend
every single day of your life.

*H*ave one friend who will always sign your permission slip to get out of the things you don't want to do.

For example:

You: "Should I go to my boss's daughter's baby shower?"

Her: "That would be completely irresponsible considering all of the great shoe sales going on."

Each night as you fall asleep, feel grateful for some way
that a friend has touched your life.

*E*very summer, meet a group of pals to watch
a sunset on the beach. Bring blankets and a picnic,
and stay to watch the stars come out.
Make wishes on the falling stars. See how many wishes have
come true next year when you meet to do it again.

Good friends are like stars.
You don't always see them,
but you know they're always there!

old saying